SAFE
in the Arms of
JESUS

SAFE
in the Arms of
JESUS

*God's Provision for
the Death of Those
Who Cannot Believe*

ROBERT P. LIGHTNER

kregel
PUBLICATIONS

Grand Rapids, MI 49501

Safe in the Arms of Jesus: God's Provision for the Death of Those Who Cannot Believe

© 2000 by Robert P. Lightner

Published by Kregel Publications, a division of Kregel, Inc., P.O. Box 2607, Grand Rapids, MI 49501. Kregel Publications provides trusted, biblical publications for Christian growth and service. Your comments and suggestions are valued.

For more information about Kregel Publications, visit our web site: www.kregel.com

Cover photo: © PhotoDisc, Inc.

ISBN 0-8254-3156-5

Printed in the United States of America

1 2 3 4 5 / 04 03 02 01 00

*To Joshua Lightner Steitz,
my namesake*

Contents

Acknowledgments

This work is based largely upon an earlier work long out of print, *Heaven for Those Who Can't Believe,* published by Regular Baptist Press. My thanks to Regular Baptist Press for their permission to have that work revised under the current title.

My thanks to all who have expressed their appreciation for the help they received from the earlier work referred to above. Letters, phone calls, and personal expressions continue to be received. It is my sincere prayer that many more will find their burden lighter and their faith stronger as a result of reading this book.

God Cares, and So Do I

Only God understands fully the pain you feel from the death of your beloved. Your family and close friends care deeply and want to help, but they hardly know how. All of our efforts seem so futile, and our words sound so empty at such a time as this.

But please be assured that God in heaven cares very much for you and about you and your loss. Through God's Word, the Bible, He wants to minister to you now. Won't you let Him?

I wish I could bring back your loved one. I wish I could take away all of your heartache and answer all of your questions, but I can't. What I can do, though, is show you from God's Word how much He loves you and wants to help you bear this burden. Based upon what the Bible says, I can tell you that your loved one is in heaven now. I can also tell you how to be sure that you will see your darling again and spend eternity with the precious one whom you have lost in death.

> Cast your burden on the Lord,
>   And He shall sustain you;
> He shall never permit the righteous
>   to be moved. (Psalm 55:22 NKJV)

But you, O Lord, are a God full of
compassion, and gracious,
Longsuffering and abundant in mercy
and truth. (Psalm 86:15 NKJV)

He cares for you. (1 Peter 5:7 NIV)

I have a good and true word for you! The one who
has been taken from you is in heaven now. This is not
an exaggerated claim. Neither is it something I am
telling you simply because I know you want to hear
it. The Bible supports this belief. It is really true. And
what is more, it is true even if you had a miscarriage
or an abortion.

Yes, your child is in heaven. You believe that, I
am sure, and hundreds of thousands of other moms
and dads have believed it about their children when
they stood in the same lonely place. But what we all
need at such a time is a sound basis for our faith, a
reason for our hope. That is what we want, isn't it?
We need some assurance that our belief is grounded
in fact. We need to know that our feelings are not
betraying us, that we are right to believe as we do.

Thank God, the Bible provides us with reasons
for believing that our loved one is safe in the arms of

Jesus. God has provided in His Word what you need
most right now.

> *Children of the heav'nly Father*
>   *safely in his bosom gather;*
> *nestling bird or star in heaven*
>   *such a refuge ne'er was given.*
>
> *God his own doth tend and nourish;*
>   *in his holy courts they flourish.*
> *From all evil things he spares them;*
>   *in his mighty arms he bears them.*
>
> *Neither life nor death shall ever*
>   *from the Lord his children sever;*
> *unto them his grace he showeth,*
>   *and their sorrows all he knoweth.*
>
> *Though he giveth or he taketh,*
>   *God his children ne'er forsaketh,*
> *his the loving purpose solely*
>   *to preserve them pure and holy.*[1]

Children
in the Bible

The words *children* and *child* appear many times in the Bible. Both the Old and the New Testaments abound with these words. From the teaching in these many references we may be sure that little ones have a definite place both in the great heart of God and in His sovereign plan.

In all of the Bible references to infants and young children, not once is there so much as a hint that they will ever be eternally lost and separated from God if they die before they have had an opportunity to respond to the gospel. There are instances in the Bible— such as when Pharaoh ordered the death of all male babies born to the Hebrews (Exod. 1:15–22)—when it would have been appropriate to include a word about their eternal abode. But not once, even when reference is made to the death of children, is there so much as a suggestion that any would suffer eternal separation from God.

Why, we ask reverently, are we never told that those who cannot respond in faith to Christ spend eternity with those who reject Him if, in fact, that were the case? In the Bible, infants, little children, and any others who cannot believe are neither told to believe nor expected to do so. They are not classified as wicked evildoers and rejecters of God's grace. It is always adults who are addressed, either directly or in-directly, regarding these matters. Because the Bible has so much to say about those who cannot believe and yet says nothing about their being eternally sepa-rated from God because of their inability, we conclude that they have heaven as their home. They die safely in the arms of Jesus.

I encourage you to put your loved one's name in the space provided in the following verse from a famous hymn.

> *Safe in the arms of Jesus,*
>   *Safe on His gentle breast,*
> *There by His love o'ershaded,*
>   *Sweetly my {_____} shall rest.*[1]

Jesus and Little Children

Throughout His earthly ministry, Jesus gave an extra measure of tender attention to children. He claimed for them a place in His kingdom. He even chose children to illustrate the fundamental character of those who would enter the kingdom of God.

Jesus took the little children in His arms and blessed them (Mark 10:13–16). What a special sight it must have been! The adults around Jesus, including His disciples, did not want the little children to annoy Him. But the Savior assured them that He was not bothered by the children; rather, He used them to illustrate the kind of spirit an adult must have to experience a place in God's kingdom.

> People were bringing little children to Jesus to have him touch them, but the disciples rebuked them. When Jesus saw this, he was indignant. He said to them, "Let the little children come to me, and do not hinder them, for the kingdom of God belongs to such as these. I tell you the truth, anyone who will not receive the kingdom of God like a little child will never enter it." And he took the children in his arms, put his hands on them and blessed them. (Mark 10:13–16 NIV)

On another occasion, Jesus told His listeners that those who welcome and receive a child in His name are welcoming and receiving Him. In fact, He even equated the children's lack of rejection of Him with faith. He spoke of them as those who "believe" in Him (Matt. 18:1–14). Boldly, the Savior told His listeners that it was not His Father's will that any of the little ones should perish (v. 14). What an assurance that is for you as you grieve your deep loss.

> At that time the disciples came to Jesus and asked, "Who is the greatest in the kingdom of heaven?"
>
> He called a little child and had him stand among them. And he said: "I tell you the truth, unless you change and become like little children, you will never enter the kingdom of heaven. Therefore, whoever humbles himself like this child is the greatest in the kingdom of heaven.
>
> And whoever welcomes a little child like this in my name welcomes me. But if anyone causes one of these little ones who believe in me to sin, it would be better for him to have a large millstone hung around

his neck and to be drowned in the depths
of the sea. . . .

See that you do not look down on one
of these little ones. For I tell you that their
angels in heaven always see the face of my
Father in heaven.

What do you think? If a man owns a
hundred sheep, and one of them wanders
away, will he not leave the ninety-nine on
the hills and go to look for the one that
wandered off? And if he finds it, I tell you
the truth, he is happier about that one sheep
than about the ninety-nine that did not
wander off. In the same way your Father in
heaven is not willing that any of these little
ones should be lost." (Matthew 18:1–6,
10–14 NIV)

During His earthly ministry, the Lord Jesus gave
much attention to children. Benjamin B. Warfield, a
great evangelical spokesman of the past, summarized
well the Savior's interest in and ministry for children:

What Jesus did for children, we may perhaps sum up as follows. He illustrated the

ideal of childhood in his own life as a child. He manifested the tenderness of his affection for children by conferring blessings upon them in every stage of their development as he was occasionally brought into contact with them. He asserted for children a recognized place in his kingdom, and dealt faithfully and lovingly with each age as it presented itself to him in the course of his work. He chose the condition of childhood as a type of the fundamental character of the recipients of the kingdom of God. He adopted the relation of childhood as the most vivid earthly image of the relation of God's people to him who was not ashamed to be called their Father which is in heaven, and thus reflected back upon this relation a glory by which it has been transfigured ever since.[1]

What does all of Christ's interest in and ministry for infants and young children mean for grieving parents and family? Because Christ was so concerned with those who could not believe and because He did so much for them during His life, we have reason to believe that He loves them and grants them eternal life when they die.

Jesus welcomed and received children when He was here on earth. He not only spoke of them as believing in Him but He also died for them. He died for all, the Bible tells us plainly. Why did He die? Jesus died to pay the debt owed to Him because of Adam's sin. When Adam sinned, the Bible teaches, he represented the whole human race, every individual ever to live on planet earth. The potential race was somehow in him, and because of this everyone has been affected by the first Adam's disobedience.

But the wonderful part of the story is that when Jesus Christ, the last Adam, died on the cross, He paid the debt brought about by sin for everyone, the same group affected by the first Adam's sin. Jesus' death fully satisfied all the demands of God's offended righteousness resulting from Adam's sin.

The reason some adults do not go to heaven is because they refuse to accept what Christ has done for them. They refuse to believe in Him as their personal Savior. But all of those who have never been able to understand, and therefore have neither accepted nor refused God's great salvation, go to heaven when they die.

Salvation is found in Christ alone. It is the substitutionary death of Christ that appeases God's anger of sin (Rom. 5:9). In His death on the cross, Jesus took upon Himself the judgment of God. For those who accept Jesus as Savior, God's righteous demands are satisfied and His anger averted. God's judgment is poured out only upon His enemies (Nah. 1:2). Those who *cannot* believe are not God's enemies. They have been "reconciled to God" (Rom. 5:10).

Surely the eternal torment of hell is a manifestation of God's wrath. Those who will experience the wrath of God in that place will do so because they rejected His love in Christ and thus deserve the consequences. Those who cannot believe cannot disbelieve either; therefore, we may be sure that they will spend eternity in heaven.

Truly, all are born in a state of condemnation. That condemnation is removed when a person responds to God's provision of grace in Christ. "He who believes in him is not judged; he who does not believe has been judged already because he has not believed in the name of the only begotten Son of God" (John 3:18).

Once more we come back to the question: What of those who cannot believe? My answer is that because the price has been paid in full, the debt is canceled until it is rejected. Therefore, God can receive into His presence all those who did not receive His Son by faith because they *could not* do so. Without violating His righteous demands in any way, these are accepted into God's presence. After all, His righteous demands were met at Calvary. The debt has been paid! Jesus paid it all! Nothing more is owed to God.

When those who can and do believe, their faith does not contribute anything toward removing the debt of sin. God's requirement of faith from the sinner is never viewed in Scripture as part of the payment toward his or her debt. The debt of sin is only charged against those who reject the payment that God the Son has made and that God the Father has accepted. Those who cannot believe owe no more to God. Those who can believe but do not, owe the full debt; that is why they cannot go to heaven. Their debt can never be paid by themselves. To refuse Christ's payment is to seal one's eternal destiny, but to be *unable to receive it* is to be covered by the payment already made and accepted by God.

The substitutionary death of Christ also provides support for believing that those who cannot believe are saved at the time of their death. Jesus did die for all. Surely those who cannot believe were not excluded from His gracious provision. As we noted earlier, Christ's death paid the full price for each person's sin. Until the Savior and His finished work are rejected, therefore, the debt remains canceled.

Another factor related to Christ's death supports this view. If those who cannot believe are not beneficiaries of God's salvation, Christ died for them in vain. Nothing whatsoever was accomplished by His work for them if they are not saved by it. Someone might ask, "But what about those who reject Christ's salvation? Of what value or to what avail was His death for them?" The answer is that Christ's death is the basis for the condemnation of those who do not believe. But surely His death is not the basis of the condemnation of those who cannot believe because they cannot and did not reject it. Scripture clearly teaches that one who does not believe is condemned for that very reason: ". . . he has not believed in the name of the only begotten Son of God" (John 3:18). God's wrath is upon those who choose not to believe: "He who believes in the Son has eternal life; but he who does not obey the Son shall not see life, but the wrath of God abides on him" (John 3:36). Only if those who cannot believe are saved does the finished work of Christ have any relation whatsoever to them.

The Character
of God

Everything we know about the God of the Bible supports the fact that heaven is the eternal home of your child and all who have died without the ability to decide for or against Christ. A number of the descriptive characteristics of God found in Scripture lend strong support to this contention. Salvation is available for all of those who cannot respond to the gospel; they are safe in heaven after death. These truths also provide comfort for you.

The characteristics or attributes of God tell us much more than that He simply acts in certain ways and does certain things. God's attributes are not merely qualities that are attached to His Person. Neither are they simply things that He does. He actually *is* each of these things. They are His essence. They describe His Person, not merely His behavior.

Without imposing human ideas on these divine characteristics, it would seem out of harmony with the very nature of God if any who cannot believe die and go to eternal judgment. Review with me some of God's attributes with this thought in mind.

God's Wisdom

God has never made a mistake, and He will never make one. Imagine that! He is the all-wise God. In wisdom He has chosen and implemented the plan of redemption that will bring the most glory to Himself. His Son is the Savior who died for all. Wisely, God has prescribed one way of salvation and only one—apart from the Lord Jesus Christ, His Son, there is no salvation. Those who reject Him as personal Savior are forever lost. They have no hope and are doomed to eternal separation from Him.

But those who *cannot* believe do not *refuse* God's offer; they do not reject Christ the Savior or God's revelation in nature and human conscience. In infinite wisdom God cares for them.

Because rejection of the Savior is the reason people will be eternally separated from God, those who do not reject Him because they are not able to make a conscious decision, enter heaven on the basis of the finished work of Christ. God's plan of redemption is wise, because He is wise.

God's Love

"God is love" is the clear revelation of Scripture (1 John 4:16). A more profound statement cannot be found in all the Bible. God not only loves but also *is* love. It seems totally out of harmony with this truth to believe that God would send to hell those who had not reached a level of mental competence enabling them to decide for the Savior. After all, God sent His Son to die for all. He loved the world enough to do that. That same love avails until such a time as it is rejected and spurned. God's infinite love for all is illustrated, supported, and strengthened when we see how in love He secures the salvation of that large company who cannot believe.

> *Jesus loves me! this I know*
> *For the Bible tells me so;*
> *Little ones to Him belong;*
> *They are weak but He is strong.*

Chorus:

> *Yes, Jesus loves me!*
> *Yes, Jesus loves me!*
> *Yes, Jesus loves me!*
> *The Bible tells me so.*

> *Jesus loves me! He who died,*
> *Heaven's gate to open wide;*
> *He will wash away my sin,*
> *Let His little child come in.*[1]

God's Mercy and Grace— Expressions of His Love

The psalmist wrote, "The LORD is compassionate and gracious, slow to anger and abounding in lovingkindness [mercy]" (Ps. 103:8). Mercy and grace may be viewed as two sides of one truth. God's mercy means deserved penalty and punishment are withheld. The grace of God refers to His giving favor to those who do not deserve it.

How do these two perfections of God relate to the eternal destiny of your loved one? They relate in this way: Both God's mercy and His grace were shown through Jesus Christ toward all—to those who can and do believe as well as those who cannot believe. The punishment for sin that every member of the human race deserves was borne by Christ. What *we* deserve, *He* received. He cannot be more merciful. What He does for mankind in salvation is based upon the mercy He revealed through His death on the cross. God's grace was displayed there as well. There, through the death of His Son, God made it possible to show favor and to save all, even though not one person deserves it. How, we must ask, could it possibly be said that God was merciful and gracious toward those who cannot believe, if, in fact, even one of that group perishes?

God's Goodness

"The L ORD is good" (Nah. 1:7). Does God do good things? Does He do only good things? To both of these questions the answer is an unqualified "yes." But could that honestly be the response to either one of the questions if He damned forever even one who could not understand and, therefore, could not meet the requirement for salvation that He Himself established?

We do not believe biblical truth only when we can find no objections to it. God calls upon us to believe His Word regardless of the problems it may create for us. The Bible does not teach the damnation of those who *cannot* believe. Instead, it teaches the goodness of God. It would seem to be highly inconsistent with His goodness if anyone who could not believe and died was forever lost. Rather, I believe that all such as these receive eternal life at the time of their death because Scripture nowhere teaches anything to the contrary and because such belief is in perfect accord with God's Person.

God's Justice

The L ORD, said Zephaniah, "will do no injustice" (Zeph. 3:5). David the psalmist expressed the same truth regarding God's justice when he said, "The L ORD performs righteous deeds and judgments for all who are oppressed" (Ps. 103:6).

Because God is just, we may be assured that He deals equitably and according to truth with all of His creatures. He is never unfair, even though it may seem so to us. But if He demanded of any of His creatures something that they could not do, would He be just? Because God has made clear in His Word that those who reject His Son as Savior will be eternally separated from Him, how would He be just in refusing into His presence those who were never *able* to receive or reject His salvation?

The Son of God came declaring God's righteousness ". . . that He might be just and the justifier of the one who has faith in Jesus" (Rom. 3:26). But there are many people who *cannot* put faith in Jesus. What will happen to them? Based upon our knowledge of God's justice and the satisfaction of His offended righteousness because of the work of His Son, we believe that He is the Justifier of those who cannot believe just as certainly as He is of those who do believe.

God's Holiness

"Holy is the LORD our God" (Ps. 99:9). "God is light, and in him there is no darkness at all" (1 John 1:5).

What about the absolute holiness of God in relation to those who cannot believe? Because God is holy and because those who cannot believe are born in sin, does it not follow that they cannot be saved?

No, it does not!

But it would most certainly be true that those who cannot believe would not receive eternal life if Christ had not died for them and paid for their sin. He needed to pay the full price demanded by God because of God's offended righteousness and He paid for all—for those who cannot believe as well as for those who can and do believe. Therefore, no one is condemned to eternal torment simply because he or she is considered to have sinned in Adam and to have been born in sin. God has done something about that sin and the guilt that resulted from it. The final and ultimate reason for eternal separation from the presence of God is the rejection of His Son as Savior. There is no other way to explain the many passages of Scripture that present faith as the one condition of salvation.

God's Wrath

The Bible says a good deal about the wrath of God. To talk of this aspect of God, however, is not popular or appealing. Even those who believe in the righeous anger of God tend to say little about it.

God's wrath must not be understood to mean His loss of self-control. His wrath is not an outburst of irrational behavior as it is with humans. Those who experience God's wrath always receive exactly what they deserve. We can understand the wrath of God by contrasting it with His love. Just as His love is the expression of an emotional attitude, so is His wrath. The difference between the two is that God's love results in favor (grace) toward the sinner, whereas His wrath results in punishment of the sinner. God's wrath is displayed toward those who spurn His love. It is an expression of His justice.

How does biblical teaching about God's wrath relate to the salvation of those who cannot believe? It relates very definitely because those who experience God's wrath deserve it. They enter into it because they refuse God's way of escape from it. Those who cannot believe have not refused God's grace. Is it the will of God to pour out His wrath on them?

God has told us clearly that the reason people do not have their names written in the Book of Life is that they obstinately and deliberately *choose* not to receive

Christ as their personal Savior. These are the ones who will be forever separated from God (Rev. 20:11–15). Personal, deliberate *rejection* of Christ is the basis for God's eternal judgment.

Be comforted to know, however, that your child, who could not reject Christ as Savior and could not oppose God by evil works, is with Jesus in heaven now.

Although God allowed death to come to your home it does not mean that He does not love you. It is helpful to remember that He allowed people to kill His Son even though His love for Him is beyond description or comparison. Through the death of Christ, God provided heaven for your child. He also has a purpose—perhaps a number of purposes—for your child's death. This truth may be hard for you to believe just now. That purpose is probably not at all clear. Trust God and He will make Himself very real to you even in this time of intense sorrow.

You might never know in this life why you have suffered such a tremendous loss. The most important thing for you to do right now, in spite of your tears, is to cling to God with all of your hurts and doubts. He will never leave you or forsake you. That is a promise to you from God Himself (Heb. 13:5).

The Biblical Basis for Eternal Judgment

I magine a vision such as the following. The apostle John saw a "great white throne" (Rev. 20:11). God was seated on the throne. Those who appeared before the throne were the unsaved dead because the saved dead were raised earlier (v. 5). All the unsaved dead of all the ages were brought to appear before Almighty God. Each one was "judged from the things which were written in the books" (v. 12). Each one was judged "according to their deeds" (v. 13). All who appeared for this judgment were "thrown into the lake of fire" because their names were not written in "the book of life" (v. 15). The reason their names were not in the Book of Life was that they had not believed; they had not received the Lord Jesus Christ as their personal Savior from sin. Their works demonstrated their lost condition and separation from God.

All who appeared before the Great White Throne were judged according to their works. In a day still to come, all who are unregenerate will first stand before God for judgment at the Great White Throne. We can be sure that those who died without ever being able to believe will not be there.

But how can we be so sure of that? They have no works, having done neither good nor evil—that is why. Clearly, the basis of judgment at this future time will be what the dead have done. Equally clear, all of and only the unregenerate will appear at this judgment. Because those who died before they could believe have no works, we may be sure that they will not appear before the Great White Throne. And because all of those outside of Christ will most certainly appear there, we may be sure that those who cannot believe will not be eternally separated from God. If they are not among the unregenerate and will not appear before God at this time, we conclude that they are among the redeemed. There most certainly is salvation for those who cannot believe! They all do go to heaven, not to hell.

CHAPTER
6

The One Way to Heaven

Those who cannot believe may have been born to Christian or non-Christian parents. They may have been born in America or in any other part of the world. Where they were born or to whom they were born makes no difference when it comes to the question of their eternal destiny.

Without doubt, the majority of Christians believe that those who cannot meet God's requirement for salvation and die in that condition are taken to safety and bliss in God's heaven. But it is probably true that few who hold such a view know in fact *why* they believe as they do. Sooner or later, to one extent or another, the problem of the eternal destiny of those who cannot believe touches most of us. It would be well for us to establish a basis for our belief before we need to face the problem ourselves, either within our own families or within the families of friends.

How many ways to heaven are there? Only one! Jesus said, "I am the way, and the truth, and the life" (John 14:6). Only one way has been opened whereby humans can be accepted by God. That one way is through His Son, the Lord Jesus Christ. He alone is the Savior; there is no other. Apart from Him there is no salvation. Sinners, regardless of age or mental ability, must be related to Jesus the Savior if they are to spend eternity in God's heaven. Unless benefits of the shed blood of the Redeemer are applied to them, they will forever remain outside of the family of God and therefore outside of heaven.

This has been the hope of those who believe the Bible. It is not by works of righteousness we have done, or could do, but by God's mercy that we are saved. This has been, and still is, the heart of biblical preaching. And that is as it should be. Salvation is not based on any human merit or effort. It is all of God! He does the saving. He brings regeneration to the sinner through Christ, by means of the Holy Spirit and the written Word of God.

It has also been the view of most evangelical Christians that there is but one condition that the sinner must meet to gain salvation in Christ. Personal faith, individual trust, is presented many times in Scripture as the only human condition for salvation. In 150 references, faith is presented as the only requirement for the sinner to be saved. "What must I do to be saved?" the Philippian jailer asked. Through the Spirit, Paul and Silas gave the divine answer: "Believe in the Lord Jesus, and you shall be saved" (Acts 16:31).

We find this throughout Scripture: Salvation is

by God's grace through man's faith in nothing less than Jesus' atoning death. And, of course, millions have experienced this great salvation. They have acknowledged themselves to be sinners and Christ to be the only Savior. They have accepted Him as their own substitute, as the one who paid the full price for all of their sins.

The Bible makes abundantly clear, too, that all are invited to come and drink of the water of life freely. The door of God's grace and mercy always stands wide open. All the sinner needs to do is receive the Savior as his or her own. There is room in heaven for as many as will obey the Spirit's call and respond to His work in their heart. No one will ever be turned away who responds by faith to God's salvation. Yes, it is truly wonderful that to as many as receive Christ as their Savior from sin, to them, all of them, God gives the right and the privilege of being His children (John 1:12).

But what about those who cannot believe and therefore cannot receive Christ as Savior? How about all of those who either die before they are capable of decision-making or who remain, as long as they live, unable to respond to God's great and grand invitation? Will all of these miss heaven because they did not respond to God's offer of grace when, in fact, they

SAFE IN THE ARMS OF JESUS

could not respond? I do not believe that for a moment. It seems to me that to believe such a thing impugns the very character of God. It is my firm conviction, rather, that all who have died without ever being capable of making a decision to receive Christ as Savior are safe in His arms nonetheless.

Those who cannot believe are never called upon by God to believe. That challenge is issued to those capable of believing. God invites those to Himself who can, in fact, respond to His invitation. Would it not be mockery for God to call upon His creatures and hold them responsible for doing what they could not do?

In all the biblical passages concerning the eternal state of the lost, only adults capable of making a decision are described. Infants and young children, and anyone who is incapable of making an intelligent choice, are never mentioned. The complete silence of Scripture regarding the presence of such people in eternal torment argues against their being there. Although this is admittedly an argument from silence, it is a compelling silence in which we can take comfort.

Over one hundred and fifty years ago, the following poem was inscribed on the tombstone of four infants. The writer of these lines struggles to understand the same questions we struggle with as well.

Beneath this stone, four infants' ashes lie;
Say, are they lost or saved?
If death's by sin, they sinned;
    because they're here;
If heaven's by works,
    in heaven they can't appear.
Reason, ah! how depraved!
Revere the sacred page, the knot's untied;
They died, for Adam sinned—
    they live, for Jesus died.[1]

CHAPTER
7

The Place
of Faith

The Lord Jesus Christ alone saves. He is the Savior. Neither good works nor faith in itself saves. In the Bible, faith in Christ is the only stated condition of salvation, but it is the condition only for those who can exercise it, not for those who cannot.

The work of the Holy Spirit of God, so indispensable to one's faith and salvation, is performed upon those who can understand and respond to it. Many people die who could not respond either by accepting God's offer of grace or by rejecting it. What is the eternal destiny of these dear ones? I believe that they are safe in the arms of Jesus. There they are overshadowed by His love for all eternity.

No serious student of Scripture doubts the necessity of personal faith in Christ for salvation by those who can exercise it. But why do people exercise faith in Christ? What motivates them to do so? Do they simply decide on their own without any outside influence? No. According to the Bible, the Holy Spirit of God has a very vital part in bringing people to see their need of the Savior and in enabling them to receive Christ as Savior. In fact, without this work of the Holy Spirit, no one would ever believe the gospel or "good news." God the Holy Spirit moves upon the stubborn will of the individual, enabling him or her to respond in faith to God's offer of salvation. Jesus spoke of this divine work on the human heart when He said, "No one can come to Me unless the Father who sent Me draws him" (John 6:44).

Nowhere in Scripture are we told that a person is lost because the Spirit of God did not move upon his will. Condemnation is always brought about by man's sin and his stubborn rebellion against God, a rebellion that climaxes in the rejection of God's Son as Savior.

The Father draws people to Himself as the Spirit of God uses Scripture to convict of sin and eventually bring life to the believing sinner (John 3:5; 1 Peter 1:23). But this ministry of the third person of the Godhead is not operative upon those who are unable to understand the Word and to respond to the claims of Christ.

Faith has no merit of its own. It adds nothing to the complete salvation provided by Christ. It is not a work. "Faith consists not in doing something but in receiving something."[1] "Faith is no more than an activity of reception contributing nothing to that which it receives."[2] The salvation God offers the sinner is an undeserved and completely unearned grace-salvation. It is always viewed in the Bible as a gift (see Eph. 2:8–9).

So, we can agree that faith has no merit of its own. But what does that have to do with the question at hand? How does this fact relate to the question of the salvation of those who cannot believe? It has much to do with it! Since faith contributes nothing, its absence in those who cannot exercise it does not hinder the sovereign God from accomplishing in them all that He does in those who can and do believe. All who can believe must do so to receive eternal life. All who cannot believe receive the same eternal life provided by Christ for them at the time of death because they are able neither to receive nor to reject it. God gives everlasting life freely to all in both groups. He justifies freely, though not in payment of anything owed to the sinner (Rom. 3:24). Because He can justify freely those who believe, He does the same for those who cannot believe.

CHAPTER 8

The Death
of a Little Child
in the King's
House

The infant son born to King David and Bathsheba died. The child had been conceived in an adulterous relationship. During the baby's illness everything was done to save the child's life, all to no avail. There was fasting, praying, and much weeping—yet the little one died. Unspeakable sorrow and grief were experienced as they always are when someone we love dearly is taken from us. Immediately after the baby died, David, the king, acknowledged that he could not bring the child back from the dead, but at the same time he knew that his baby was in heaven and that he would one day go to be with the child.

You can have the same assurance today that David had, assurance that your loved one is safe in heaven.

David, the man after God's own heart, had sinned grievously. He was guilty of adultery and murder. According to the law he deserved death! But because he honestly acknowledged his sin, confessed it, and did not harden his heart against the Lord, the just penalty was not carried out against him.

Because of David's sin the enemies of the people of God, who were also the enemies of God Himself, blasphemed Israel's God. Shame and reproach were brought upon God and His people. Our sins always seem to have a way of affecting many other people. In some way, God's honor and justice had to be displayed before His enemies. That is why "the LORD struck the child that Uriah's widow bore to David, so that he was very sick" (2 Sam. 12:15).

David was brought to his senses by the word of God through Nathan. The task God gave to Nathan was a difficult one indeed. Later, when David was alone, he poured out his heart to God and prayed that the child would be restored. But his request was not granted. On the seventh day, the child died (2 Sam. 12:18). The servants debated what to do. They gathered to plan their strategy. David saw them, heard them whispering, and supposed rightly that the child had died. He then stopped fasting and praying; he washed and anointed himself and worshiped the Lord (vv. 19–20). The servants could not understand his sudden change of behavior. They asked him about it. David's reply constitutes one of the great texts of Scripture in support of the salvation of those not capable of believing.

> And he said, "While the child was *still* alive,
> I fasted and wept; for I said, 'Who knows,
> the LORD may be gracious to me, that the
> child may live.' But now he has died; why

should I fast? Can I bring him back again?
I shall go to him, but he will not return to
me." (2 Samuel 12:22–23, italics mine)

Life after death was a certainty for David. That he
would be with his son again in the future was his firm
belief. He never doubted that fact for a moment. David
was rightly related to the Lord, and he did not question that he would spend eternity with Him. Nor did
he have any doubt that his infant son, taken in death
before he could decide for or against his father's God,
would be there also.

Some people argue that David's declaration meant
merely that he would one day join his son in death.
As the child had died, so would the father in due time.
But such a view does not account for the anticipated
reunion and fellowship with his son that is strongly
implied in the statement and in the context. David's
act of worship in the house of the Lord is inexplicable
if the death of his son merely reminded David of his
own certain death.

Neither does this weak explanation account for
David's contrasting attitude when his other son,
Absalom, died. After Absalom became a man he rebelled
against God and sinned terribly. He even attempted

to seize his father's kingdom, but was killed in battle. When David heard of his son's death, he was grief-stricken. He wept bitterly. In fact, he even wished he could have died instead of his son (2 Sam. 18:33). Clearly, David was not at all certain of Absalom's relation to God and therefore of his future—hence his grief and weeping. But of the infant son who died, he was sure. So certain was David of the child's eternal home that he knew he would go to be with him. This assurance allowed him to turn from grief to worshipful prayer.

> It was this thought of reunion with his dead child which cheered David; but where did he think the reunion would be? In the grave? In hell? In heaven? He believed that he himself would go to heaven after death and consequently meant to express the belief that his child had but gone on before him to that blessed abode. The idea of meeting his child in the unconscious grave could not have rationally comforted him; nor could the thought of meeting him in hell have cheered his spirit; but the thought of

meeting him in heaven had in itself the
power of turning his weeping into joy.[1]

I dearly love a little child,
  And Jesus loved young children too!
He ever sweetly on them smiled,
  And placed them with His chosen few.

When cradled on his mother's breast,
  A babe was brought to Jesus' feet
He laid His hand upon his head,
  And blessed it with a promise sweet.

"Forbid them not," the Savior said,
  "Oh suffer them to come to Me,
Of such my heavenly kingdom is—
  Like them may all of my followers be."

Young children are the gems of earth,
  The brightest jewels mothers have.
They sparkle on the throbbing breast
  But brighter shine beyond the grave.[2]

*Questions
Parents Ask*

I t is usually easier to ask questions than it is to answer them. Doubtless this study has raised some questions for you. Parents who have lost a child probably have more questions than can be discussed here. I have tried, however, to think of major problems related to this topic and have also approached others to hear their questions. The following are, I believe, the ones most frequently asked or thought about with respect to the eternal destiny of those who cannot believe.

We must guard against dogmatism in our answers. Scripture does not always deal with the questions we have. Whether God has chosen to give us the information we want or not, our complete confidence and trust must be in Him. Hopefully, the following discussion will be helpful in increasing our understanding of several difficult issues.

What About Those Whom the Gospel Has Not Reached?

If those who are incapable of making a decision receive eternal life at death, what about those who at the time of death are capable of making such a decision but have never heard the good news of salvation? Do not the reasons for believing in the salvation of the first group also apply to the second? I think not, for the following reasons.

God has given to all a revelation of Himself in both nature and conscience (Ps. 19:1–6; Rom. 1:20); therefore, all adults are without excuse. Even where the gospel and the name of Christ have not been heard, God's revelation in nature and in conscience has been given. Paul described those who rejected God's general revelation and God's response to this rejection: He gave them up (Rom. 1:24–32). God reveals truth to an open heart. When humans reject the lesser revelation of God in nature and conscience, they are demonstrating their rejection also of God's greater revelation in Christ.

In places where the gospel has not reached, God holds people responsible for receiving the revelation He has given them. When they receive it, I believe He in sovereign grace sees to it that they hear the good news of salvation in Christ alone so they can believe and be saved. Response to God's message in nature and conscience does not bring salvation, but it does reveal a willingness to respond to God. It gives evidence of an open and receptive heart.

When a person who lives in a land where the gospel is not heard reaches the point when he or she can respond to God's revelation in nature and in conscience, that person is no longer one who cannot believe. From that point on the person becomes responsible for what is done with what is known.

Those who are unable to respond to God's revelation in nature or to His Son have His salvation applied to them at the time of death, whether they live where the gospel has reached or where it has not.

What Happens to Preborn Children Lost Through Miscarriage or Abortion?

One of the most difficult experiences expectant parents might face is the loss of a child through miscarriage. Looking forward to the birth of a child, the beginning of a new life, and the love that will be shared with that child is a precious, exciting experience. A miscarriage robs the parents of those joys, and my heart goes out to all parents who have been through that difficult experience.

Based on what the Scriptures teach about God's intent for human life and what we know today about the human fetus, I believe that a fetus is a person. I believe that the life of an individual person, known and loved by God, begins at the moment of conception. As such, God cares for that human life in just the same way He cares for the infant who dies or the older child or adult who was not able to make a conscious decision to receive Christ. God applies the finished work of Christ to those people. He accepts them into His presence because of Christ's death for them, and they are safe in the arms of Jesus.

Abortion results in the death of a person, not the mere loss of a formless bit of human tissue. In some very exceptional cases, a doctor may have to choose between the life of an unborn child and the life of the mother. The vast majority of abortions today, however, are performed because mothers (and fathers) choose to end the life of their unborn child without any morally defensible reasons for doing so. Thousands and thousands of women have made this choice and lived to regret their actions. Many of them have come to know that in spite of their choice, God loves them. And they have found forgiveness and peace only by turning in faith to Christ.

Just as God cares for those babies who die through miscarriage, I believe that God cares for those lost through abortion. The choice of abortion does not change the fact that God graciously cares for those who cannot believe. They are safe in the arms of Jesus at the time of their death.

What About Guardian Angels?

Nowhere in Scripture does the term "guardian angels" appear. This does not mean, of course, that such beings do not exist. The term usually refers to the holy angels assigned by God to watch over infants and young children. Christian artists have often visualized this concept for us.

Scripture clearly teaches the existence of holy angels. Angels are spirit beings who are messengers of God. Worship and service of God are their chief functions. As "ministering spirits sent forth to minister for them who shall be heirs of salvation" (Heb. 1:14 KJV), these angelic emissaries have, as their special assignment, to watch and care for the children of God (1 Kings 19:5; Ps. 91:11; Dan. 6:22; Matt. 2:13, 19; Acts 5:19).

The question is not, Do angels minister to those who will be heirs of salvation? Scripture plainly says that they do (Heb. 1:14). Rather, the question is, When does this ministry begin? No definite starting point for this work is given. It would seem natural, however, for it to begin as soon as life begins. If it did not begin then, we would expect to be told when it did.

Whether one angel (or more) is assigned to each individual infant, or whether there is simply a general ministry of watching and caring by all of the holy angels over these little ones, is difficult to say. We may be sure, though, that angels perform a ministry upon all of those who are heirs of salvation.

What Are Infants Like in Heaven?

In this book, we have been setting forth and defending the view that all who cannot believe receive eternal life when they die. The question is often raised, "What will these individuals be like in heaven?" Will infants and young children, for example, be infants and young children there? Anxious parents often ask pastors, loved ones, or close friends, "Will I see my baby in heaven?" Some students of Scripture believe that infants and children will be such in heaven. J. Vernon McGee states it this way:

> Will our children be as we last saw them? I do not know nor can I prove it from Scripture (for Scripture is silent at this point), but I believe with all my heart that God will raise the little ones as such, and the mother's arms that have ached for them will have the opportunity of holding them. The father's hand that never held the little hand

will be given that privilege. I believe that
the little ones will grow up in heaven in
the care of their earthly parents—if they
[the parents] are saved.[1]

That we will know our loved ones in heaven is
certain. In our future life with God, there will be in-
creased knowledge. Surely we will not know and rec-
ognize less then than we do now. But whether babies
will also be babies in heaven is another question.

From general biblical information, we know that
age will not be a factor in heaven. Very likely everyone will be the same in age and maturity. We do not
know, of course, what that age will be. We do know
one thing, however, that helps us answer the question
before us. Throughout eternity, all of heaven's
occupants will give God endless praise and worship
(Ps. 48:1; Phil. 4:20; Heb. 13:21). This means, of
course, that all will need to be old enough to do so.

Whether parents will have their babies as babies in
heaven is not really the most important thing. Heaven
will be wonderful because the Lord is there. Jesus rose
from the grave in a physical body. He was recognized
and touched. In that same body He ascended back to
the Father. When He comes for His own, they will be

like Him (1 John 3:2). That means that all of heaven's occupants will be known. It follows, therefore, that all who are in heaven will be recognizable.

What if My Baby Was Not Baptized?

The meaning of water baptism is determined, to a large extent, by what is believed about baptizing babies. Those who view baptism as a gift of God, an effective and actual offer of divine life, believe, of course, that infants should be baptized. Why not? Adherents of this view would agree with Kurt Marquart's belief: ". . . Why deprive poor little babies of this wonderful blessing? And, after all, as sinful human beings they need this heavenly, life-giving bath."[2]

On the other hand, those who understand water baptism in the New Testament to be an outward sign of an inward work of grace—a visible testimony symbolizing one's death, burial, and resurrection with Christ—believe that it is both unnecessary and unscriptural to baptize babies.

Those who think that infants should be baptized see the rite as the New Testament counterpart of circumcision in the Old Testament. No passage of Scripture states this, however. They also appeal, for biblical support of their view, to such passages as Acts 2:39. Peter said to the Jews, "The promise is unto you, and to your children" (KJV). Christ's words, "Let the little children come to me, and do not hinder them" (Matt. 19:14 NIV), are also used in support of infant baptism. None of the Scripture passages used to support this doctrine truly do so. Louis Berkhof defends infant baptism in his *Systematic Theology.* Yet even he states, "It may be said at the outset that there is no explicit command in a single instance in which we are plainly told that children were baptized."[3]

It is generally agreed today, among students of history and of the Bible, that infant baptism arose around A.D. 200. The practice is based largely upon tradition rather than statements of Scripture. No biblical teaching exhorts the baptizing of babies.

More importantly, salvation is not imparted to anyone through water baptism. No one—adult or infant—ever had or ever will have salvation through the waters of baptism, whether the amount of water used be little or much. All who are delivered from the wrath to come are delivered through Christ alone. Only He can and does save the soul.

When Are Those Who Cannot Believe Saved?

We have learned from Scripture that at birth all are guilty before God. No one is right with God. All are in need of divine life. All need Christ's work applied to them. The Bible does not tell us precisely when salvation comes to those who cannot believe. We may be assured only that they do spend eternity with God in heaven. It seems logical to conclude that their salvation comes at the point of death.

Has God Chosen All Who Will Die Before They Can Believe?

The Bible teaches clearly that God makes the first move in the salvation of an individual. God has chosen us "in him before the creation of the world" (Eph. 1:4 NIV). God "predestined us to be adopted as sons through Jesus Christ, in accordance with his pleasure and will" (Eph. 1:5 NIV). Peter wrote that believers were "chosen according to the foreknowledge of God the Father" (1 Peter 1:2 NIV). And yet, it is not the choice of God in eternity past that brings eternal life to the sinner. That life comes only when the finished work of Christ is applied to the individual. Scripture everywhere affirms that there must be an appropriation by the individual of the finished work of Christ before salvation comes. God in sovereign grace does this for those who cannot believe at the time of death.

The question is, Are all those who die before they are capable of decision-making chosen by God to be saved? Since, as we have discovered in our study thus far, the biblical evidence supports the salvation of those who cannot believe, we must conclude that all such individuals are chosen by God for salvation. No one will be in heaven who was not so chosen, not given to Jesus by the Father (John 6:37).

All of those who die before they can believe are in heaven; therefore, they are among those who have been given to Jesus by the Father. We conclude, then, that under the sovereign hand of God all who die before they can believe are chosen by Him to be heirs of salvation. He does know all things, the end from the beginning. He alone gives and takes life. Because He is good and does all things well, this conclusion is based solidly upon and is in complete harmony with His holy Person.

What Is the Age of Accountability?

We could just as easily put the question this way: At what age is belief in Christ possible? No definite answer can be given. The age will not be the same for everyone. To be sure, all who are mentally sound do reach a point in their lives when they become fully responsible to God for their actions. There are many opinions as to when that point is reached. And that is all they are—opinions. The Bible does not give us the answer to this question. James 4:17 comes the closest of any passage, but it gives no specific age: "Therefore to him that knoweth to do good, and doeth it not, to him it is sin" (KJV).

Perhaps God did not give us an "age of account-ability" because there is no one age for all. Then, too, had He given a specific age, we would probably not be concerned about children hearing the gospel before that time.

There are many testimonies from those who were saved at an early age, but not all young children are capable of decision-making. Much depends on the child's mental ability and training. Jonathan Edwards, America's great Puritan preacher, for example, was saved at eight years of age. Richard Baxter, the great English preacher, was born again at the age of six. The well-known hymn writer Isaac Watts came to faith in Christ when he was nine.

This is a comforting hope for those who have lost in death a little one or one who was not mentally competent. If there was no ability or capability to understand and therefore to accept or to reject the claims of Christ, we may be sure that all such people are safe in the arms of Jesus.

What Will Happen When the Lord Returns for His Own?

When the Lord returns, the dead in Christ—those who have had His finished work applied to them and are therefore members of His body—will be resurrected. They will be joined, to meet the Lord in the air, by living saints, those who have also had Christ's finished work applied to them (1 Thess. 4:13–18). The dead will come forth from the grave with glorified bodies. That is, they will have bodies that will not age or decay. They will be incorruptible and immortal. Those who are alive when all of this takes place will also be changed. They, too, will receive glorified bodies, but without experiencing physical death (1 Cor. 15:51–58). All who meet the Lord will be made like Him. They will receive glorified bodies when they see Him as He is (1 John 3:2). "Death is swallowed up in victory. O death, where is thy sting? O grave, where is thy victory?" (1 Cor. 15:54–55 KJV).

The question before us is, What about those who cannot believe who are on the earth when the Lord returns for His own? Some aspects of this question have no definite scriptural answer. The Bible simply does not tell us in so many words how those who cannot believe will be related to this great event. However, we may certainly assume some things based upon what we have discovered about the eternal destiny of those who cannot believe.

Those who have died without being able to believe will most certainly be raised along with all the others in Christ. The problems relate to those living but unable to believe and also to infants still in their mother's womb. What will happen to these individuals when Jesus comes?

The Bible teaches that individual life begins at the time of conception. Parents pass on to their child both their material and their immaterial parts—the spirit, soul, and body. All of the individual's genes and chromosomes, along with all genetic information, are present at the time of conception. There are even some hints of prenatal consciousness in the Bible (see Gen. 25:22–23; Luke 1:41, 44).

The pregnant women who are saved will be caught up (raptured) when Jesus comes for His own. It is reasonable to believe that their unborn children will share in the physical transformation that takes place at the Lord's coming. What of pregnant women who are not saved? They will not be changed but will remain on the earth to endure the time of the Great Tribulation (Rev. 6–19). And what about their unborn infants?

We know that there will be great suffering on the earth as it experiences a time of unparalled tribulation. Jesus specifically mentioned expectant mothers when he spoke of it (Matt. 24:19). Regardless of their mothers' choices not to accept Christ, all children born during the tribulation period are protected by grace. They are no different than other children who are not able to believe.

What about those who cannot believe, who are living when the Lord returns, and who have saved parents? Will the parents be taken to be with the Lord and the children left on earth? I think not! Because those who are living at the Lord's return will experience a spiritual translation instead of physical death, it seems reasonable to conclude that all of those who are incapable of believing will be caught up to be with the Lord in just the same way as all of those who have trusted Jesus Christ as their personal Savior. I do not believe God will divide families by taking the parents to be with Him and leaving their children who cannot believe to endure His wrath in the Tribulation. To be sure, there will be separations when the Lord returns, but they will be between those who have trusted Christ and those who have not trusted Him. It is unlikely that the separation will be between saved parents and their children who are unable to believe.

> *Beside a grave I knelt in tears,*
> *   and felt a presence as I prayed.*
> *I turned to Jesus standing near—*
> *   He said: "Be not afraid!"*
>
> *"Lord, You have conquered death, I know;*
> *   restore again to life," I said,*
> *"This little one that we loved so—"*
> *   He said: "She is not dead!"*
>
> *"Not dead? "That thought small comfort gives,*
> *   our emptied arms can't hold her near.*
> *Now far way with You she lives—"*
> *   He said: "But I am here!"*

"She is not lost who lives in You?
Grief says such things can never be.
Yet hope asks what the heart must do—"
He said: "Abide in Me!"

—based on a poem
by Rossiter W. Raymond

CHAPTER 10

Parent Talk

Praise be to the God and Father of our
Lord Jesus Christ, the Father of compassion
and the God of all comfort, who comforts
us in all our troubles, so that we can
comfort those in any trouble with the comfort we ourselves have received from God.
(2 Corinthians 1:3–4 NIV)

The apostle Paul wrote these words to God's people
in their time of grief. They are also meant for
grieving moms and dads who had accepted Christ as
their Savior.

Although your little one, taken from you in death,
is now with God in heaven, there is doubtless an aching
void in your broken heart. That is perfectly normal
and understandable. Surely only those who have lost
in death one of their own flesh and blood know how
hard such a loss is. Now as never before you need and
want assurance and comfort from God. Empty, pious
words that somehow put the burden of recovery on
yourselves or others leave you cold and unmoved.

"Hang in there."

"There's a rainbow after the storm."

"We're pulling for you."

These and similar well-meaning words may even increase your remorse and grief in the hours and days of loneliness.

What you need is a word from your heavenly Father. As hard as it may be to do, you must, if you want relief for your anguished soul, be assured that God is good. As Robert T. Ketcham put it so well when he was deep in sorrow over the death of his loved one, "Your heavenly Father is too good to be unkind and too wise to make mistakes."

That is what Nahum the prophet said of God, too. Right in the midst of describing God's mighty power, His anger at sin, and the certainty of His future judgment, Nahum penned these words: "The LORD is good, a strong hold in the day of trouble; and he knoweth them that trust in him" (Nah. 1:7 KJV). The psalmist expressed the same fact about God when he said of Him, "Thou art good, and doest good; teach me thy statutes" (Ps. 119:68 KJV). Throughout the Bible, the truth of God's goodness is made known. You need to lay hold of that truth by faith.

God does not make mistakes. It may not seem like it now, but God is still in control. Your child's death was not an accident from the divine point of view. In His infinite wisdom and love your heavenly Father allowed your beloved to die. In His own way and time He will work out what you have experienced for His own glory and your good (Rom. 8:28). He knows it all, including your heartache and bitter tears. He not only knows but also cares! He cares for *you* (1 Peter 5:7).

Someone who knew how it hurts to lose a loved one asked and answered the natural question correctly:

> *Does Jesus care when I have said "good-by"*
> *To the dearest on earth to me,*
> *And my sad heart aches, till it nearly breaks,*
> *Is it aught to Him? Does He see?*
>
> *Oh yes, He cares, I know He cares,*
> *His heart is touched with my grief;*
> *When the days are weary, the long night dreary,*
> *I know my Savior cares.*[1]

Now that your dearest treasure is in heaven, that place that Jesus has prepared for you will mean more to you than ever. Your heavenly Father wants you to lean heavily upon Him always. He is strong. He can and will bear you up, so rely on Him. Take your heavy burden to Him and leave it with Him. Talk it all over with Him. Tell Him exactly how you feel. He loves you with an everlasting love. Come to Him just as you are with all of your doubts and all of your pain, anxiety, care, fears, and frustrations.

Perhaps as never before you will see, through this experience, that God is indeed sovereign. He does have the full right to do as He deems best. We are only His stewards and not really owners of His gifts to us. Perhaps this experience has given you occasion to examine yourself and your values in life. Some things that you thought mattered really do not matter very much after all. The death of that one who could not believe has no doubt reminded you of the need to submit more fully to God. Follow those good impulses and give yourself to Him completely.

When a heartache strikes—such as the death of a loved one—generally one of two things happen. Either bitterness sets in and grows into hardness of heart, or the experience helps to bolster faith and develop maturity. We have to choose which it will be. It is normal to ask God, "Why did this happen to me?" And it is not wrong to ask, "why?" But it is even better to ask, "What do You want me to learn from this difficult experience?" If you keep asking *why*, you might find yourself becoming bitter. But when you ask *what*, you will be paving the way for growth.

The ideal is for us to be so well-grounded in the faith and in our love and trust of God that every experience of life strengthens rather than disables our faith. It would be extremely wise to prepare for heartache before it comes by embracing the truth of God's goodness and wisdom. The positive experiences of life are the best times to get to know God. Then, when we find ourselves deep in the valley of despair, the going will be easier and the burdens lighter to bear. We will know from experience that God is with us—in all times.

Many Christians do not take advantage of opportunities to know God before troubles and trials strike. What can you do if your world crumbles around you and you are totally unprepared? There is still hope! God's invitation is still extended to His children. Never does He turn a deaf ear to the faintest cry from His own. Although we cannot understand why we have been called upon to pass through deep waters, we need to accept the Bible's testimony of God's goodness, love, and wisdom.

Despite all of your doubts, fears, and sorrow, rest in God, your heavenly Father. We must all admit that we do not understand many of God's ways, but through the darkest hours and the deepest waters it is so important that we keep our eyes on Him. God is not unkind; He is infinitely good and infinitely wise. Lay hold of this truth, and remind Satan of it when he bombards you with doubts and fears.

Try as best you can to learn and profit from your experience for God's glory. Seek to receive from God what He intends for you in your loss. He took your loved one because He needed another choice jewel in heaven.

> I am with you always, even to the end of the age. (Matthew 28:20)

> And the Lord, He is the one who goes before you. He will be with you, He will not leave you nor forsake you; do not fear nor be dismayed. (Deuteronomy 31:8 NKJV)

Marilyn McGinnis, a mother who lost a tiny baby in death, admitted that the adjustment was very difficult. She suggested the following four steps to help make it easier:

> The first step is to face the child's death without bitterness. Blaming God won't help matters. It only makes things worse.

Many things happen in this world that we don't understand at the time, but we have the assurance that everything fits into God's plan for our lives. . . . The second step is to ask God to use your loss for His glory. You'll be amazed at the results. . . . The third step is to be alert to ways you can help someone else who may have suffered a similar loss. . . . The fourth step is to allow yourself the healing quality of grief. Cry as long as you need to. God gave you tears for a reason. But when you've finished crying, stop. Daily visits to the cemetery and endless brooding about the life that has been taken from you will do more harm than good. Prolonged grief eventually becomes neurotic.[2]

Do not be afraid to cry. Remember that Jesus wept, too, at the death of His friend, Lazarus. Grief expressed has a healing quality. Cry until you are finished and then stop. The more quickly you can get on with life and reach out to others, the better for you. You cannot change the past; none of us can. But we can all learn from it and go on to face the future.

Perhaps God wants you to be more faithful in

rearing your remaining children in a committed, Christian home. Do your family members know the Lord as personal Savior? Ask God to use you to bring the gospel to them and to other children you know who are old enough to understand their need to accept Jesus Christ. See that all the members of your family who can believe know that they must believe before they can receive eternal life. Why not follow the practical instruction Moses gave to the children of Israel:

> And you shall love the LORD your God with
> all your heart and with all your soul and
> with all your might. And these words,
> which I am commanding you today, shall
> be on your heart; and you shall teach them
> diligently to your sons and shall talk of them
> when you sit in your house and when you
> walk by the way and when you lie down and
> when you rise up. (Deuteronomy 6:5–7)

Do not wait for a more convenient season to present the gospel to your children. You will know, perhaps better than anyone else, when they are able to understand that they are sinners. Christ alone is the way to salvation, and they must personally accept Him as their own Savior, their substitute for sin. Ask God for wisdom to know the right time and the proper way to present the claims of Christ to your children.

A friend, Frances Saville, sent me the following item. I have been unable to learn when or where it was first published. All I know is that it was written by eight-year-old Danny Dutton in response to an assignment to write an essay on "God."

A Child's Eye View of God

One of God's main jobs is making people. He makes these to put in place of the ones that die, so there will be enough people to take care of things here on earth. He doesn't make grown-ups. Just babies. I think because they are smaller and easier to make. That way He doesn't have to take up His valuable time teaching them to talk and walk. He can just leave that up to mothers and fathers. I think it works out pretty good.

God's second most important job is listening to prayers. An awful lot of this goes on, as some people like preachers, pray other times besides bedtime. God doesn't have time to listen to the radio or TV on account of this. He hears everything, not only prayers, there must be a terrible lot of noise going on in His ears, unless He has thought of a way of turning it off.

God sees everything and hears everything and is everywhere. Which keeps Him pretty busy. So you shouldn't go wasting His time going over your parent's head and ask for something they said you couldn't have.

Jesus is God's Son. He used to do all the hard work, like walking on water and doing miracles and trying to teach people about God who didn't want to learn. They finally got tired of His preaching and they crucified Him. Because He was good and kind like His Father, and He told His Father that they didn't know what they were doing and to forgive them, and God said OK. His Father appreciated everything He had done and all His hard work on earth, so He told Him He didn't have to go out on the road anymore. He could just stay in heaven. So He did. And now He helps His Father out by listening to prayers. You can pray anytime you want and they are sure to hear you because they've got it worked out so one of them is on duty all the time.

You should always go to Sunday School because it makes God happy, and if there's anybody you want to make happy, it's God. Don't skip Sunday School to do something you think will be more fun like going to the beach. This is wrong. Besides the sun doesn't come out at the beach until noon. If you don't believe in God, besides being an Atheist, you will be very lonely because your parents can't go everywhere with you like to camp but God can. It's good to know He is around when you're scared of the dark and when you can't swim very good and you get thrown in real deep water by big kids. But you shouldn't just think of what God can do for you. I figure God put me here and He can take me back anytime He pleases. And that's why I believe in God.

What a wonderful privilege we have, as moms and dads, to explain to our children what God is really like and how they can know Jesus as their Savior and friend.

Heaven
and You

They are not dead, those loved ones who have passed
  Beyond our vision for a little while.
They have but reached the Light while we still grope
  In darkness where we cannot see them smile.

They are not dead. Theirs is the fuller life,
  Theirs is the victory, the joy, the gain;
For us is still the waiting and the strife,
  For us the loneliness, for us the pain.

Then let us gird us once again with hope
  And give them smile for smile the while we wait;
And loving, serving, when our Father calls,
  We'll go to find our loved ones wait us at the gate.[1]

I t is comforting to think of our loved ones waiting for us "at the gate." But what if you are a parent who has never accepted Christ as your substitute for sin? You need to know that, according to the Bible, there is only one way of salvation! God demands perfection. To get into heaven, you must be as good as God. Impossible, you say. You are right! In and of ourselves we can never meet God's high standard. No single good work nor all the possible combined good works that we might do could ever make us fit for heaven. All people are sinners by nature and by choice. All people are born with the taint of inherited sin and guilt. Paul the apostle put it this way: "As it is written, There is none righteous, no, not one: There is none that understandeth, there is none that seeketh after God. They are all gone out of the way, they are together become unprofitable; there is none that doeth good, no, not one" (Rom. 3:10–12 KJV).

The wages of sin is death (Rom. 6:23). What is the solution, then, to this seemingly hopeless state? Jesus Christ is the solution! He is the sinless One Who gave Himself as a sacrifice for you. "And that he died for all, that they which live should not henceforth live unto themselves, but unto him which died for them, and rose again" (2 Cor. 5:15 KJV).

He died for you! God the Father is satisfied. He accepted the substitutionary death of His Son as the full payment for your sin. As a demonstration of His acceptance, He brought Jesus back from the dead. Salvation and eternal life will be yours when you place your trust in the Lord Jesus Christ as your own personal Savior, your own substitute for sin. "Yet to all who received him, to those who believed in his name, he gave the right to become children of God" (John 1:12 NIV).

Christ bore your sin in His own body on the tree. Will you accept His gracious offer of salvation and forgiveness? "For it is by grace you have been saved, through faith—and this not from yourselves, it is the gift of God—not by works, so that no one can boast" (Eph. 2:8–9 NIV).

Your loved one who could not believe and who died is in heaven now. Those who die before they can respond to God's great offer of salvation are safe in His tender care because of the finished work of Christ on their behalf. But when people reach the age when they have the ability to respond positively to the gospel, they will be eternally lost if they do not do so. "Whoever believes in him is not condemned, but whoever does not believe stands condemned already because he has not believed in the name of God's one and only Son" (John 3:18 NIV).

You will be forever separated from God, from all that is holy and good, as well as from your loved one, unless you personally accept the Lord Jesus Christ as your own Savior. Do not put off this most important decision. Tomorrow may be too late. Today is the day of salvation. Your loved one, the darling of your heart, longs to have you share with him or her the eternal bliss and happiness of heaven. Come as you are to the Savior. Do not try to make yourself ready for His presence before you come. He wants you to come to Him, and He will fit you for heaven, where your little one is now.

Weary travelers are encouraged when they see a sign in a motel or restaurant saying, "Come as your are." To weary souls burdened by sin and the trials of life, the Lord Jesus extends that same word of welcome, too: "Come as you are." If you want to see your loved one again, do not turn down His gracious offer of salvation.

> *Just as I am, without one plea*
> *But that Thy blood was shed for me,*
> *And that Thou bid'st me come to Thee,*
> *O Lamb of God, I come! I come!*

> *Just as I am, and waiting not*
> *To rid my soul of one dark blot,*
> *To Thee whose blood can cleanse each spot,*
> *O Lamb of God, I come! I come!*

> *Just as I am, though tossed about*
> *With many a conflict, many a doubt,*
> *Fightings and fears within, without,*
> *O Lamb of God, I come! I come!*

> *Just as I am, Thou wilt receive,*
> *Wilt welcome, pardon, cleanse, relieve,*
> *Because Thy promise I believe,*
> *O Lamb of God, I come! I come!*[2]

Endnotes

Chapter 1: God Cares, and So Do I

1. Original Swedish text by Caroline V. Sandell Berg (c. 1850), translated by Ernst W. Olson, 1925.

Chapter 2: Children in the Bible

1. Fanny J. Crosby, "Safe in the Arms of Jesus," *Inspiring Hymns,* comp. Al Smith (Grand Rapids, Mich.: Singspiration, 1951), 437.

Chapter 3: Jesus and Little Children

1. John E. Meeter, ed., *Selected Shorter Writings of Benjamin B. Warfield* (Nutley, N.J.: Presbyterian and Reformed Publishing Company, 1970), 1:224.

Chapter 4: The Character of God

1. Anna B. Warner, alt., "Jesus Loves Me," *Inspiring Hymns,* 454.

Chapter 6: The One Way to Heaven

1. John Bruce, *A Cypress Wreath for an Infant's Grave* (London: Hamilton Adams, 1830), 141.

Chapter 7: The Place of Faith

1. J. Gresham Machen, *What Is Faith?* (Grand Rapids, Mich.: Eerdmans, 1925), 172.
2. J. I. Packer, *Fundamentalism and the Word of God* (Grand Rapids, Mich.: Eerdmans, 1960), 172.

Chapter 8: The Death of a Little Child in the King's House

1. R. A. Webb, *The Theology of Infant Salvation* (Clarksville, Tenn.: Presbyterian Committee of Publication, 1907), 20–21.
    Still others who do believe that David was acknowledging the presence of his child in heaven argue that the child was there because he was a child of the covenant. Those who embrace this view believe that only the infants who have regenerate parents and who have received infant baptism (the New Testament sign of the covenant, they say) will go to heaven if they die. I think such a view lacks a solid scriptural base.

2.   Thomas Smyth, *Solace for Bereaved Parents* (New York: Robert Carter, 1848), 217.

Chapter 9: Questions Parents Ask

1.   J. Vernon McGee, *Death of a Little Child* (Pasadena, Calif.: Through the Bible Radio, 1970), 20.
2.   Kurt Marquart, *Christian News,* 10 September 1973.
3.   Louis Berkhof, *Systematic Theology* (Grand Rapids, Mich.: Eerdmans, 1968), 632.

Chapter 10: Parent Talk

1.   Frank E. Graeff, "Does Jesus Care?" *Inspiring Hymns,* 321.
2.   Marilyn McGinnis, "When Death Took Our Baby," *Moody Monthly,* October 1974, 50.

Chapter 11: Heaven and You

1.   J. B. Marchbanks, *Your Little One Is in Heaven* (Neptune, N.J.: Loizeaux Brothers, 1951), 25.
2.   Charlotte Elliott, "Just As I Am," *Inspiring Hymns,* 198.